Earth's Land, Air, and Water

by Emily McKenzie

PEARSON
Scott
Foresman

DK

What are natural resources?

Natural resources come from Earth. A **natural resource** is something that people can use that comes from nature. Sun, water, and air are natural resources.

Some natural resources can get used up.
Oil and coal are resources that get used up.

Some natural resources can be replaced.
We can plant new trees.

Some natural resources cannot be used up.
Sun, water, and air cannot be used up.

Water and Air

Water is a natural resource.
Plants and animals need water to live.

People need water too.
People use water to drink, cook, and clean.

Ponds and rivers have fresh water.
Oceans have salt water.

Air is a natural resource too.
Plants, animals, and people need air.
Wind is air that moves.

What are rocks and soil like?

Rocks are natural resources.
Rocks can be big or small.
A **boulder** is a very big rock.

Wind, rain, and ice can break up rocks.
Sand is made of small pieces of rock.

People use sand to make roads.
People use rocks to make houses.

Rocks are made up of **minerals.**
Minerals are a natural resource.

Gold and silver are minerals.
Quartz is a mineral.
People make glass from quartz.

Quartz

Soil

Soil covers most of the land.
Soil is a natural resource.
Soil is made of clay, sand, and humus.
It also has air and water in it.

Some animals live in soil.
Different plants grow in different kinds
of soil.

Sandy soil is rough and dry.
Clay soil is soft and smooth.
Humus is a part of soil that comes from living things.

Sand

Clay

Humus

How do people use plants?

Plants are natural resources.
People use plants for many things.
People use wood to build homes and to
make paper.

This T-shirt is made from a cotton plant.
People use wheat to make bread.

How does Earth change?

Earth changes all the time.
Water and wind move rocks and soil.
This is called **erosion.**

Plants can stop erosion.
Their roots keep soil in place.

Weather can change Earth.
Water can break up rocks.
This is called **weathering.**

Animals can change Earth.
They dig homes and break up the soil.

How can people help protect Earth?

People can change Earth.
People can harm the land, air, and water.
This is called **pollution.**

Pollution hurts plants and animals.
People try to stop pollution.
People want to keep Earth clean.
They want to keep plants and animals safe.

Reduce, Reuse, Recycle

Trash is a kind of pollution.
When we pick up trash, we help stop pollution.

People can recycle trash.
To **recycle** means to change something so that it can be used again.

Did you know milk cartons can be recycled? The milk cartons in this picture were used to make a playground!

People can reuse things to stop pollution.
To reuse means to use over and over again.

People can reduce the natural resources
they use.
To reduce means to use less.

Protecting Plants and Animals

People cut down trees.

Animals live in the trees.

The animals lose their homes.

People can plant new trees for the animals.

Forests change all the time.
Trees can burn in forest fires.
The wind can blow down trees.
New trees take a long time to grow back.

People must be careful with campfires.
Campfires can start a forest fire.
Forest fires can kill many trees and animals.

Plants and animals can also lose their homes when people build where they live.

A refuge is a safe place for plants
and animals.
People can visit a refuge and enjoy all the
plants and animals living in it.

Earth gives us many natural resources.
Let's enjoy them and help keep them safe!

Glossary

boulder   a large rock

erosion   when wind and rain move soil

minerals   natural resources that make up rocks

natural resource   something people use that comes from nature

pollution   putting harmful things into the water, air, or land

recycle   to change something so it can be used again

sand   small pieces of rock

weathering   when water or temperature change the land